In the Name of Allah,
the Most Gracious,
the Most Merciful

1.

The Sound That Never Halts in Muslim Cities

2.

The Islamic Athan

3.

A Wonderful Story
A 180 Degrees Turn

4.

Does Taking the Time to Worship God Through Prayer Reduce **Productivity?**

5.

How Did **the Story of the Athan Start?**

6.

The Virtue of the Muathan

7.

Prayer
The Great Pillar of Islam

8.

Lafcadio Hearn and
Bilal ibn Rabah

9.

The Detailed Translation
of the Athan

The Sound That **Never Halts** in Muslim Cities

When someone takes a stroll in any Muslim city of the world, he/she can't help but to notice the mosques with their long minarets and the call that radiates from them amongst the bustling city, full of life. It is as if this call is the indicator of the wheel of life and the scale used to measure people's livelihoods. Gérard de Nerval states in his book, Voyage to the

Orient, **"The very first time I heard the harmonic and flawless sound of the caller to prayer, I was totally overtaken by an indescribable feeling. I asked the translator: What is the caller saying? He replied: He is announcing that none is worthy of worship other than God. I then said: What is he saying next? The translator replied: He is calling the asleep to wake up by saying, 'Thee who sleeps be dependent on He Who is Ever-Living and doesn't sleep.'"** So what is this call, and what is its story?

The Muslim
Athan

The athan (call to prayer) has a huge significance with Muslims. Its sound sends security, calmness and joy into the souls of those who hear it. Their desire to listen to the athan never ceases despite hearing it time and time again. The call reminds Muslims of the five obligatory prayers, which is one of the most important commands of God Almighty. The reason for this importance is to prevent the Muslims' connection with their Lord from being interrupted.

The athan serves as a reminder for Muslims to carry out what God Almighty has decreed and to prevent getting caught up in the worldly affairs of the temporary world.

There is no reason to be bothered by the soft, soulful sound that is a statement of God's Mightiness and Oneness. The Muslims repeat the athan as it is being called, so that the deep meanings of the athan may become established in their self-conscious and share the athan's virtue with its caller. The call which the faithful people rush to answer and ill-hearted creatures flee from, is mentioned by the Prophet Muhammad, may the mercy and blessings of God be upon him, said, **"When the athan is pronounced Satan takes to his heels (and flees)… in order not to hear the athan."** (Al Bukahri # 608). Author, Edward William Lane, mentions in his book, (An Account of the Manner and Customs of the Modern Egyptians): **"The sound of the athan is totally wondrous,**

especially in the calmness of the night."

During the time of Prophet Muhammad, may the mercy and blessings of God be upon him, God informed us about a nation of people, whom used to make fun of the caller to prayer whenever the prayer would be called. This was considered making fun of both the athan and the prayer, which are considered acts of worship. The reason for their actions was their lack of respect and foolishness, which led to the ignorance towards the truth and unsavory mocking. Had this group used common sense or the least level of thoughtfulness, then they would have given the athan and its glorious meanings, deeper thought and not dared to carry out such disrespectful acts and behavior.

A Wonderful Story

A 180 Degrees Turn

At the time of Prophet Muhammad, may the mercy and blessings of God be upon him, there was a group of youth whom whenever they would hear the call to prayer, would imitate and make fun of it. Muhammad, may the mercy and blessings of God be upon him, heard them and said, **"Who did I hear his voice was raised?"** To which they pointed to a teen known as "Aba Mahtoora". The Prophet dismissed the others but told Aba

Mahtoora to remain. The Prophet intended to develop Aba Mahthoora's talented voice, for the gift of the Almighty should be used for positive causes to benefit him and all people, instead for unfavorable use. The Prophet said, **"Go ahead and call for prayer"**, then taught him the words of the athan, then mentioned, **"May God bless you."** As a result, God guided Aba Mahthoora to Islam and he became the "muathan (the one who calls to prayer) of the Prophet in Mecca. This is the story of how Aba Mahthoora started as a disbeliever, who made fun and mockery of the athan, but ended as a truthful believer and the Muathan of the Prophet, may the mercy and blessings of God be upon him. (Musnad Ahmad # 15380).

Does Taking the Time to Worship God Through Prayer Reduce **Productivity?**

The athan and performing the prayer creates no conflict when it comes to meeting the needs of daily activities, as humans desire to meet their worldly needs. Athan and prayer take very short time to perform and the positive aspects of prayer includes becoming closer to God and renewing the spiritual energy in helping to refrain from immoral behavior. Since the prayer takes minimal time there is plenty of time left in the day to carry out the lawful worldly acts.

People who have never responded to a call of prayer or gone to a mosque might imagine contradictions between spiritual and physical needs. It is safe to say that there is no such contradictions in Islam.

On the contrary, spiritual needs assists in completing physical needs and vice versa. Those who are able to balance the two aspects, will be less affected by daily conflicts and grief, therefore have greater capabilities at increasing productivity in daily affairs. Those who are able to successfully balance the physical needs with the spiritual needs will be rewarded greatly in the Hereafter, as mentioned in the Qur'an. "O you who have believed, when [the adhan] is called for the prayer on the day of Jumu'ah [Friday], then proceed to the remembrance of Allah and leave trade. That is better for you, if you only knew."

"And when the prayer has been concluded, disperse within the land and seek from the bounty of Allah , and remember Allah often that you may succeed." (Qur'an 10;62:9)

How Did the Story of the Athan Start?

Initially, the Prophet - may the mercy and blessings of God be upon him - and the companions couldn't make the call for prayer in Mecca, as the pagans would harass them. Instead they would pray secretly, depending on their circumstances. Some Muslims prayed in the paths or their homes, either individually or in pairs, so that the pagans wouldn't have the opportunity to harm them. However, after they migrated to Al Medina, the group prayer was made obligatory, therefore, the group would estimate the prayer times and attend the mosque and pray together. Initially this was a challenge for the Muslims, as some would estimate the time of prayer earlier than others, and would have to wait and hence miss carrying out amends, while others would be late and hence would miss the allocated prayer time.

One day the Prophet, may the mercy and blessings of God be upon him, sat with his companions and discussed how the prayer time should be announced. So the noble companions contemplated the logical options of their time, which led to suggestions including using a bell similar to the Christians, blowing a trumpet as Jews were accustomed, and lighting a fire and raising a flag at the time of prayer. However, none of these ideas were accepted by the Prophet, may the mercy and blessings of God be upon him. That same night a companion named, Abdullah ibn Zaid had a dream, in which a man visited him and taught him the words of the athan. The companion rushed to the Prophet and told him about the dream, to which the Prophet said, **"It is a true dream."** The Prophet then told him to teach the words of the athan to another companion, known as Bilal ibn Rabah, as Bilal had a deep, loud voice. From that moment the rite of the Muslim athan began and until this very moment its sound doesn't halt around the globe. (Abu Dawoud # 498)

The **Virtue** of
the Muathan

Due to the importance of the message of the athan, the "muathan has a high position and will receive great reward from God. It is the muathan who reminds the forgetful and brings activity into those who are lazy to attend the prayer. The muathan gains the reward of the worshipers who attend the prayer after having heard the athan. The Prophet, may the mercy and blessings of

God be upon him, informed us that if people knew of the virtue of the athan and its high status, that they would all race to be the one to call to prayer, even if the winner would be decided by drawing straws (Al Bukhari # 615); and for that reason Omar ibn Al-Khattab, the 2nd Muslim caliph, wished that he would have been the muathan and would have been if it weren't for his given responsibilities as Caliph. (Al Bauhaqi # 2041)

Prayer

The Great Pillar of Islam

The high status of the athan lies in the content of what it calls to. The prayer is the 2nd pillar of worship in Islam and how a Muslim is differentiated from people of other faiths. Prayer in Islam is similar to the pillar that holds the roof of a building and protects it from collapsing altogether. In prayer, a Muslim can find total comfort from the daily worries and hardships and can call directly upon his Lord. Only by performing the prayer devoutly and calmly, can one find complete peace and spiritual satisfaction and is practiced and known by the majority of Muslims around the world. For this reason the Prophet, may the mercy and blessings of God be upon him, used to say to Bilal, his muathan **"O Bilal, call for prayer, [and] let it bring comfort to us."** (Abu Dawooud # 4985). Hence, a believer feels comfort by performing prayer not by leaving it and nothing is more evident of this than the fact that Muslims are committed to carrying out this act of worship day and night, in the manner, method and number that their Prophet taught to them, over 1400 years ago.

Lafcadio Hearn
on
Bilal ibn Rabah

The author, Lafcadio Hearn, wrote a short article on the first muadan in Islam (Bilal ibn Rabah) in which he stated, **"Bilal the (colored) Abyssinian, whose voice was the mightiest and sweetest in Islam. In those first days Bilal was persecuted as a slave of the persecuted Prophet of God. And in the 'Gulistan' it is told how he suffered. But after our (Prophet) had departed into the chamber of Allah and the tawny** horsemen of the desert had ridden from Mecca even to the gates of India... and the young crescent of Islam, slender as a sword, had waxed into a vast moon of glory that filled the world, Bilal still lived with a wonderful health of years given unto the people of his race. But he sang only for the Caliph. And the Caliph was Omar. So one day it came to pass that the people of Damascus whither Omar had travelled on a visit begged the Caliph saying: 'O Commander of the Faithful, we pray that thee ask Bilal to sing the call to prayer for us even as it was taught him by our (Prophet) Mohammed.' Now Bilal was nearly a century old, but his voice was deep and sweet as ever. And they aided him to ascent the minaret..."

The Detailed Translation of the Athan

This magnificent call has great meanings that become apparent for whoever thinks about it. The athan encourages one to put aside worldly distractions and activities, turn to God and reach a state of spiritual happiness; for all things that have a worldly value, God is greater than those. It isn't logical that a Muslim be preoccupied with this world and not be preoccupied with Who is greater!! The athan consists of six repeated sentences, which are outlined in the following:

God is the greatest, God is the greatest: This is said four times and is an opening-phrase that makes one ask themselves questions!! The phrase doesn't inform one what is it that God is greater than!! That is because you may complete the sentence by adding absolutely any word... For God is greater that everything and anything... God is greater than anything you may be doing at the time of the calling to prayer, therefore, you must leave (unless in emergency) anything you are doing whenever God is calling to you.

I bear witness that none is worthy of worship other than God:

If you truly believe that none has the right to be worshipped other than God then you would worship God alone. You wouldn't worship your job and desire success or lust. Worship isn't merely movements of the body that are performed, instead it is obeying God above everything else. When a Muslim bears witness that none is worthy of worship except for God Alone, he/she believes that worshiping God Almighty is the greatest value in his/her life and that without it there is no meaning to life.

I bear witness that Muhammad, may the mercy and blessings of God be upon him, is the final Messenger of God:

Which means that Muhammad is the Messenger of God who was sent to the entire world. There were also previous messengers, including: Noah, Abraham, Moses and Jesus, may the mercy and blessings of God be upon them. The message of all the messengers was based on calling humankind to the previous phrase of athan: **(I bear witness that none is worthy of worship other than God).**

Come to Prayer:

Here the muathan is encouraging you to immediately come to perform the prayer, for prayer is a pause from worldly materialistic pastimes and an establishment of a direct link between servant and his/her Lord.

Rich and poor, white and colored, young and old, all of whom gather together at a mosque to pray together. Prayer is a mandate of all Prophets because it brings peace and calmness that helps one get through life and accept what God Almighty has destined for him/her with an accepting and reassuring attitude.

Come to Success:

This means come and rush to what leads to your success and triumph. God has created mankind so that they may worship and glorify Him, and whenever a person fulfills this worship of God Alone he/she reaches that ultimate success, which is entering Paradise in the Hereafter. The Paradise in the Hereafter is the success that all other losses compared to are negligible, and any sacrifice towards it is miniscule in comparison to its reward. It is the Paradise of the Most Merciful that should be the goal of every person on the face of this planet. For if a soul were to lose out on Paradise then what would be the value of anything else on earth?!

God is the greatest... God is the greatest... I bear witness that none is worthy of worship other than God:

Just as the muathan started with stating that God is the greatest and that He is One, he ends the athan in the same manner; this noble meaning remains cemented in the hearts of the believers, so that nothing from the worldly pleasures may distract them from responding to it, as everything other than God Almighty will come to an end.

The Greatest Phrase

Humanity was Created to Fulfill its Meaning

The greatest words created for humanity is: (None has the right to be worshipped other than God). This magnificent and everlasting statement is the message and first pillar of Islam: **To worship, submit and obey God Alone, Who has no partner.** This statement is the reason why God Almighty created humankind, sent down the Holy Books and sent the messengers. Whenever the muathan declares that none has the right to be worship except for God, he is announcing to the entire world the everlasting message of monotheism. The message is that God ordered humankind to say and act upon the athan, so that they may succeed in this life and in the Hereafter. The athan is the call from God that is repeated to the listeners, enters one's heart and communicates with one's soul about its truth and details, so that one may exit distractions and darkness to find certainty and complete light in this life and in the Hereafter. So become from those who respond to its call and become from the successful!

CPSIA information can be obtained
at www.ICGtesting.com
Printed in the USA
BVHW052329050223
657834BV00013B/2329